ANTRIN THOCHTS
on
AULDEN DAYS

Recollections of Life in Huntly
80 years Ago

W. Gordon McPherson

Bennachie Publishing
Oldmeldrum
1996

1

This collection first published in August 1996
Reprint in November 1996
by

Bennachie Publishing, Oldmeldrum

ISBN 0 9526972 1 1

Published on behalf of **HUNTLY Ltd.**
with funding support from
Gordon Forum for the Arts
and
European Union, LEADER II Programme

Printed by Highland Printers, Henderson Road, Inverness

CONTENTS

PREFACE

In this booklet I have put together some of my recollections of life in Huntly as it was seventy to eighty years ago, before the advent of electricity and the ubiquitous petrol engine transformed everyday life so profoundly.

It is hard to believe that up to the period of which I write people in general were living at the same pace as their forbears did for centuries - the pace of the horse!
I speak of course of everday life in the town and the country.

This is in no sense an autobiography, although the intrusive "I" may unavoidably creep in; nor is it an exact history of the town. I have just let my memory to roam up and down the time-span of approximately 1912 to 1925, the aim being to show some of the changes in Huntly between then and now.

The account is not comprehensive, but sufficient is recorded, I think, for the purpose intended.

Acknowledgement

I am grateful for the encouragement and the financial assistance given to this project by the Gordon Forum for the Arts.
I am indebted to Mrs P. Goodall for slaving over a hot computer and to Miss Margaret Dempster for sharing her extensive knowledge of Huntly.

Introduction

Having read and enjoyed the book of poems in the Doric called "Antrin Thochts", I felt privileged to be asked to write the introduction to this latest publication by W. Gordon McPherson. He has gathered together his memories of things long ago, of his early life in Huntly from around eighty or so years ago.

The result is an extraordinary collection of vivid images. Here you will find stories of 'Feein Markets' and 'Term Days', fishwives with wicker creels, the circus coming to town, milk cairts, gigs and hurleys. W. Gordon McPherson indicates that, "I have drawn pictures with words, writing entirely from memory. I think that these stories will appeal to the older generation, and to young people too; in fact to all who are interested in their local history." This is most surely true. It is a written record of our valuable heritage.

It is most educational in a way that is easy to absorb. Indeed, I sense that this work will have a much wider appeal. W. Gordon McPherson feels this too. "If you changed the name of the town and the names of the people, the businesses and the shops," he says, "you'd find that it was not just about Huntly. It is the story of any country town in the North East of Scotland."

For those young and old there are things to be recalled with fondness or learned afresh. How do you play with 'nicklers' and 'dolders'? Where was the Rush where the salmon leapt? What was 'plunky'? How did the Foggie Dirder get its name? What did the call "A.B.C.R.L." mean, when sledging on the factory brae?

Very soon, all will be revealed, as you are transported back in time.

John Swan, Rector,
The Gordon Schools,
 Huntly

Also published for W. Gordon McPherson
by **Bennachie Publishing**

"ANTRIN THOCHTS"

A delightful book of Doric poems and stories

Antrin Thochts
on
Aulden Days

Recollections of Life in Huntly
80 Years Ago

EARLY DAYS

I was born in Granary Street in 1907 and I suppose the first sound I heard , apart from my own bawling , would have been the "dird-dird" of the big hammer in "Sellar's Smiddy".

Sellar's was a big concern in the Town , employing many "Smiddiers" making agricultural implements used all over the Country - "Sellar's Ploos" were famous.

A story was told of "Aul Sellar" and the foreman testing out a plough :
"That's it ! said the foreman , "She's as gweed as ony in the country ."
"As gweed's nae ese ," said Sellar , "she his ti be better nor ony ither ploo in the country !"

The Smiddy , with its forges and tall chimney stack , was on the south side of the street where the Hanover Housing is now - on the other side was the open stockyard for finished implements and repair work and so on .

The big empty building , still there , was the store .

There were no safety helmets or eye shields in those days - it was a common sight to see a Smiddier standing outside with his back to the wall , having a steel splinter picked out of his eye by the expert needle of Tom Henderson .

It was a great blow to the Town when Sellar 's flitted to Alloa to be nearer coal and steel suppliers .

School

There were just the three buildings in those days - the original Duchess of Gordon building , the Elementary - now the Community Centre (Linden Centre) - and the Secondary.

The Primary was on the right side of the Bow , the Supplementary on the left , coming from the Square.

We went to the Primary first , of course , then to the Elementary , where we sat the "Qualifying Exam", then we were "streamed" - the word they use now , I believe - to either the Secondary or the Supplementary.

The "Supps" were supposed to be better with their hands .

The Secondary went on to take their "Highers" and thence to the University.

In the Primary we learned by rote , just repeated things until they were thoroughly stuck in our heads.

Our start in literature was the A.B.C. - on a stand hung a book rather like a paper pattern book , on each page of which was a letter appropriately illustrated . The leaves were turned as we mastered each letter. "A for the Apple ! we chanted, "B for the Bat and the Ball !" and so on .

During the Great War (1914 - 18) we got slates and slate pencils to save paper.

On the outside wall on the left as you go into the present Primary School door , there is a ledge about a foot from the groud .

When the bell was rung and we gathered in a line to get in , we sharpened our pencils on that ledge , and if you look you'll see the groove worn out by the children of my generation , a reminder of the Great War.

As we got on a bit we had Copy Books - emphasis was placed on writing well and legibly .
I don't know if Copy Books are still used in School , but judging from adult writing I see , I should not . Much of the writing now is quite unintelligible ; such writing I regard as illiterate .

We knitted scarves too, and picked sphagnum moss - we got a heap on our desks and picked out the bits of grass, heather twigs and whatnot from it. This moss was said to have great healing properties on wounds, but I question now if it was ever used - we did it, I think, to keep up civilian morale.

There was no organised Sport at School, mostly scratch games of Football and Cricket among ourselves with an occasional Match with, maybe, Keith.

We had to buy our own Football too, and anyone with a bat brought it along.

No organised School Sports either.

"Bools" was a great craze now and again - we went to school with a bagful.

One of the games was with a "Dolder" - an oversized Boolie, - a button was put on top, the opponent let "fung" at it, and if he knocked it off he got a boolie, and if he didn't he lost his.

Dolder owners were the Plutocrats of the playground.

"Nicklers" were much more coveted and never played with - these were extra brown, and highly glossy ones.

The young girls did a lot of skipping; the reason, probably, why we have so many spritely mature Ladies in the Town?

The boys' dress, well into the Secondary, was shorts, boots usually, a jacket and a jersey in Winter. All my time at school I never had a coat or a cap and I think the others were mostly the same.

When about 15 or 16 some of us ventured into "langers", to the envy of the rest.

There were no School Dinners in those days as we know them noe, but there was soup available made by Miss Rae in the School Kitchen.

We ran home for ours; scholars from the country (some biked in, some came by train) very often had a bottle of milk and a "piece".

No school buses, of course.

Discipline was strict, but not hard - we were just taught to behave in a civilised way.

There was one notable thing about school, or more precisely, after it - when you left School you had a job to go to, though it was only errand boy to a shop - there were many more shops then. Several of my friends left for that - they ended up with businesses of their own. There were many more apprentice-ships too.

Mr. James was headmaster when I was at school - very profes-sional, grey swallow-tail - very correct ; when he retired he shook hands with every scholar as we filed past him in the School Hall - I saw the tears in his eyes; the School was his life.

All sorts of theories of education have been tried since then, groups, open classrooms, etc., and found wanting. I believe ours was the best and simplest.

SHOPS

Shopping was a bit different in the '20s - there were many more shops and of course no supermarkets.

Suppose you were sent up, say to Watt Brothers (now Alldays) for some messages, as I was often - usually when I had some other ploy on hand. When you went in, there were probably more customers, so you just waited your turn. Everything was served over the counter and you usually had time for a "news".

You wanted maybe, a pound of sugar; a brown paper bag was put on the scales, a pound weight was put on the other side, then the shopkeeper went to a bin, took out a scoopful and poured it into the bag until the scale went down; the bag was tied round with string ("meerchan twine"), which was kept in a tin box on the counter with a cutter on top.
Rice, semolina and suchlike were all loose - practically nothing was packed; even cigarette packets were "bare". "Bogie Roll" tobacco was sold by chopping off a bit from a coil like a rope.

In the Butcher's shop there was just the wooden counter and the scales.
Against the wall at the back the meat hung on hooks - legs, sides and all the rest. The butcher just carved what you wanted from what you saw. Summer must have been a trial for butchers before electricity came in - no fridges or deepfreezes.
Some articles you never see in a butcher's shop now, which were plentiful in those days - fly-papers hanging from the ceiling; and it was obvious why they were there!
You never see a fly or a 'blue-bottle now.
The bakers' shops are not very different, only more packaged stuff now.

The first time I went into Donald's, after I came back to stay here, I rather 'dumfoonert the quines' by asking for a sixpence's worth of 'fardin hard'. That's the name they always got, although they were, I think, a ha'penny in my day - in old money of course.Shop baked biscuits were loose, no packets.

The money used was of course the old Sterling - two hundred and forty pennies to the pound. In the 1914-18 war farthings were introduced. You might have seen goods priced at, say, 1/11 d, where nowadays they might say £1. 99 - just to make things look cheaper.

In the bookseller's now there is an extraordinary choice of magazines - every sport and hobby has its weekly or monthly magazine. A feature now is the very extensive range of Anniversary cards; Birthdays, Mother's Day, Father's Day, and so on. There were none such in my day, just Christmas and New Year cards.

That, I find, is one of the biggest differences between now and then of seventy or eighty years ago - the great choice of goods now available and of course the supermarkets, unknown then.

Shops, and houses and streets, were lit by coal gas from the Gasworks in Gladstone Road.

Many shops sent vans out into the country, as the majority of farm wives had no means of getting to town, there being few cars.
One thing remains the same of course - you have to pay for what you get, but there seems now to be an awful lot more money to do it with.

INDUSTRY

There were several important industries in the town eighty years ago, now unhappily gone.

Sellars, of which I have already written, was a large employer of men; it was a great loss to the town when it went to Alloa. Spences, at the tap o the toon, produced the highest class of knitwear, sold in the best shops in the south, produced by a large staff of mainly female workers. It was a sad day when Spences closed, no doubt owing to competition from goods produced by cheap labour in the Far East.

The Mart (the Central Mart in the 1920s) was a source of considerable income to the town. Mart day was Wednesday and on that day the farmers and their wives flocked into town; many had gigs and these were parked all over the place, the Royal Oak stables were full, the gigs being parked in the closs. We had two in Granary street.
There were few cars and no cattle floats; the streets from early morning "steerin" with cattle and sheep being driven in on the hoof. Householders left their doors and gates open at their peril! In droving you had a man in front, a man behind, and as many loons as you could get hold of to guard the side streets. While the men were at the Mart the wives were doing the weekly shopping taking in, maybe, butter and eggs for barter.
Wednesday was a busy day for the shops.

A spin-off from the Mart were the three "Killin hooses" (abattoirs now!), one at the junction of Deveron Street and George Street owned by Barron and Dufton; John Rhind's near the Bogie Brig, and one at Princes Street used by Gordon Rhind and Charlie Anderson.

As a spin-off from these there was a tannery (always pronounced 'Tanneree') in Church Street between Victoria Road and Settrington Street.The hides were carried through the streets to the Tanneree heaped on a hurley.

There was a Dairy in the town, in Meadow Street, owned by Peter Reid.

The town ,as I have said, was lit by coal gas produced by the Gas Company, situated on the junction of Queen Street and Gladstone Road where the Queen's Gardens housing complex now stands. The huge gasometer was a feature of the landscape down there, not to everybody's liking.

The Licht Mannie came along to light the street lamps with a long pole which had some long-burning stuff on the end of it; he lifted a flap on the glass cover, turned the jet and lit the gas. Compared with now the town was poorly lit, but having no comparison we did not think so at the time.

There was a Dye Works down by the Bogie Brig, still working in my time, and opposite on the other side of the river, Stephen's Woollen Mills which had a shop round the corner on the Station Road.There was a weir, now dismantled, always called "The Rush" above Stephen's Mill to divert the river into lades which serviced the Wool Mill and the Dye Works.

It was a great sight after a spate in the 'Backend' to see the salmon attempting to get over the Rush. Time after time they tried; we gave a cheer when one made it at last and slipped over into the'Missies', the quiet pool above.

Up the river, by the bridge down from Bleachfield Street, was Yule's Meal Mill; on the other side of the road was Morrison's Sawmill, now a caravan park.

I always associate the sweet warm smell of a Meal Mill with the rising and falling buzz of Willie's circular saw.

Half a mile up the Bogie from the Meal Mill was Brander's Woollen Mill which made blankets. The whole process was done there; you put down the fleeces and took home the blankets. I might observe that the process of washing and degreasing reduced the wool to half its weight.

SERVICES

There were few cars in the early 1920s, no buses, no big lorries; the horse was still the means of getting there and back.
Goods came by train, the station was very busy then with eight clerks at one time, and were carried up to the shops by Wordies lorries, their office and stables were in Bogie Street where the plumbers, MacDonald, is now.

Another transport was from the Gordon Arms Hotel. Johnnie Ewen, the Porter, carried up the travellers hampers of samples from the station to the hotel on a horse-lorry.

For the passengers there was Jimmy Mearns' horse-cab, which plied between the station and the town; we used to pinch a 'hurl' up the street sitting on the back axle - unknown to Jimmy of course. Our unkind pals would then shout "Whip behind !" whereupon Jimmy would try to get at us with his long whip.

Every week the dust cairt came round to empty the 'aise-backets'. What we looked forward to was the 'water-cairt' which toured the strets occasionally in a hot summer to lay the 'stue'. This cairt was a tank with a kind of rooser at the back; great for the loons who followed 'barfit' in the spray.

16

I must explain that the roads were innocent of tar and when the wind rose so did the stue. All the carts were drawn by horse of course.

Funerals were very impressive; black-edged cards with the intimation were put in the shop windows; the hearse was drawn by two black horses with plumes on their heads, the mourners walking behind to the cemetery. Blinds were drawn along the route. Practically all funerals were from the house.The horses and hearse were the property of Mr Sandison, Strathbogie Hotel.

Cars began to come in just before the 1914 - 18 War. My father, who was a Veterinary Surgeon, had one of the first, a Renault two-seater, open of course - no doors; a hood like a pram drawn over and held by straps in front; oil lamps, later changed to acetylene. I have a distinct recollection of the smiddiers from Sellar's standing round about it in the closs when it newly arrived; this would have been about 1912-13. Previous to the car he did his rounds on horseback.

The first bus to Aberdeen was run by Benton of the Richmond Arms, Rhynie; it started off from the Square in front of the Commercial Bank (where the Royal is now); the fare I think was ten shillings return. This would have been about the mid 1920s.

A famous bus was the "Foggie Dirder" which plied between Huntly and Aberchirder. Its route to the square was via Bogie Street, Gladstone Road, Victoria Road, Upper Kirkgate and Gordon Street. The reason for this roundabout route was to avoid the horse traffic in Duke Street - the horses were somewhat alarmed by its noisy progress.

A passenger in the Dirder would understand how it acquired that soubriquet - it had solid tyres and the roads, to put it mildly, were not smooth.

The cricket pitch was rolled by horse roller; the horse had big leather pads over his hooves to prevent cutting into the turf.

Horses, like cars, need servicing; there were two blacksmiths in the town; Wilson in Deveron Street and Shearer in McVeigh Street.When we were in school in the Elementary with the classroom windows open on a hot summer's day we could hear the ring of the hammer on the anvil coming from Shearer's smiddy .

Tradesmen, painters, plumbers, carpenters, etc. going to a job, carried their gear on a hurley. My grandfather, George Mitchell, was a painter; he did a job at Artloch School once and all his stuff was rowed there and back on the hurley.

Coal was delivered by a horse lorry in one hundredweight bags. Jock Martin was our coalman.

In some houses in Huntly you will notice a low door, level with the pavement; this opened into the cellar. The coal was coupt on the pavement and shovelled through. We had this at 12 Granary Street; stone steps led down from a passage in the house to the cellar.

We used to have a mail service three times a day, and moreover the postie looked like a postie, with uniform and a peaked cap. There were few telephones; urgent messages were sent by telegram, so we had the Telegram Boy with his little round hattie and his red bike.

The late 'Darkie' Gordon was a complete master of the bicycle; he could do anything on it. I saw him once circling the statue on the Square, standing on the saddle, arms folded, a feat one would have thought impossible.
(There were no cars stanced there then!)

We had a delivery of milk to the door; Doddie Donald with his horse and milk cart with two big cans and brass taps. He blew a whistle to announce his arrival. You went out with a jug and got what quantity you wanted

I have bitter memories of that horse; like everything else he had to obey the laws of physiology and he invariably chose to do so in front of our door! I had the job of clearing up!
Jessie Paterson from the Toll also came round with milk.

Another service we had was a Town Crier, in the person of Bobby Imlach and his bell. His was not an impressive figure such as we sometimes see on TV; he was smallish and bent and wore a well-worn long grey jacket topped by a hat. He had the most abundant crop of grey whiskers - we never saw his face. His job was to go round the crossroads, ring his bell and bawl out the intimations which generally had to do with cutting off the water for a while, or some such thing.
Nobody ever understood a word he said, so we ran about until we found some-one who did know what was afoot.

Amongst the services we must count the fish-wives, who came in from the little fishing ports by train, dropping off at country stations, like Gartly and Kennethmont; from there they did their rounds on foot, comimg back to the station at the end of their round. Woe betide the Stationmaster who let the train go without them!

19

I never heard of one who dared, however late she was!

They were a hardy lot 'wi tongues it wid clip clouts'. They wore the most voluminous clothes, heaven knows how many layers, with an apron in front; from the depths somewhere in there they produced their purse, usually a black leather affair covered with scales

Their stance in Huntly on a Wednesday, market day, was at the Royal Oak, at the corner where the telephone kiosk is now.

We must not forget the butter and egg cairts which travelled from the town shops with groceries to barter for farm produce with the farm wives. A notable van was that of Adam Slorach, Butcher. He announced his coming with a horn and it is said that when the horn sounded all the dogs within earshot gathered round. He had a board sticking out at the back of the van on which the meat was sliced up... - hygene did not rank high in Adam's priorities!

SPORT

Sport in the pre-20s was not nearly so organised as it is now. Football was played on the 'Market Meer' with the crowd just standing around. A tin boxie went round for a collection - the expenses would not have been high. I suppose there was a Secretary, but no Manager, Coach, transfer fees , wages and all the rest of what seems essential now.

There was a Pavilion, if you could dignify it by that name; a little wooden affair big enough for changing in. It stood against the west wall of the Muir but was later burned down.

In the 1920s we had a "Trades League" of youths, for which the various trades in the town entered a team.

There was a very good Junior team at the Tap o the Toon who called themselves the "Magpies"; they had a black and white strip

These games on the Muir would have been just after the 1914-18 war and I suppose were mostly friendlies; the Huntly Express reports marches against, amongst others, Portsoy, Rhynie and a "Spences' Eleven".

One game sticks in my mind - a game with Buckie in 1919, when a Buckie player got a broken leg; he disputed a ball with "Beelie" Fraser who was a soutar with Alexander and came off worst - Beelie was no push-over. A broken leg! This was great excitement for the loons!

We had a fine cricket team in the twenties; I need not detail their exploits here - Patrick Scott has dealt with that very thoroughly in his *History of the Huntly Cricket Club*.

What I remember of these days is the large crowds that attended the matches, home and away; five hundred in a train to Aberdeen to see a cuptie! - these were the glory days.

There was no fence round the schoolside of the field nor much in the way of seating - just a plank laid across a post at each end.

The team were heroes to 'hiz' loons' and we looked up to them as I suppose the present generation looks up to pop stars and footballers.

I think we had better models.

Everyone has a mannerism ; John Scott on his way to the wicket always stopped halfway, bent down, plucked a blade of grass and put it between his teeth.We boys used to wait for that.

The story went round amongst us that John once hit the tower clock with a sixer, but maybe that was apocryphal. He was a mighty hitter, though!

The cricket Pavilion, like all the rest, was a very modest wooden affair compared to the modern up-to-date one.
Some good cricketers came down these old steps, though.

A golfer today would feel very deprived if he were restricted to the few clubs thought sufficient in the 20s; a *Driver*, a *Brassie* (for the second shot - balls did not fly so far), a *mid Iron*, a *Mashie* (number five or six), a *Niblick* (a number eight) and a *Putter* were thought sufficient.

No trolley either; you just carried your clubs in a "pencil" bag.

Worst deprivation of all, (some may think?) no handy pint at the end of the round!

The Course was nine holes then.

LEISURE

I wonder what the youth of today would think if they were suddenly deproved of their TV, radio, tape-recorder and such?

I suppose they would just have to make their own entertainment, as we had to do

We had the Cinema of course - "The Palais de Luxe" which we always spoke of as 'The Palace'. The building is now "Cost Cutter", before that Anton's Furniture Showroom.

On Saturday afternoons there was a Matinee for the youth which cost us, I think ,tuppence for the front seats ("the Fourpennies") which cost fourpence for adults at the usual times. It was usually packed with loons and the din was fearful; Jock Paterson, the manager, used to come among us laying into the wall with his stick, demanding, "silence in the front seats!"

He never got it!

At the piano was Meg Guthrie - she was cheered when she came in - who looked up at the screen and played appropriate music; stirring stuff for the cowboys; soulful for the mush as we thought it.

On the Saturdays when we hadn't tuppence we might go to "the Fishing" or maybe up to the Torry to play cricket, often with improvised implements, or just went on the haik somewhere to find what amusement we could; there was little money about then.

There were no buildings west of King Street at that time, just fields; the Torry itself was rough ground with plenty of whins about.

The first building to go up would have been the Gordon Cleaning Company, where Somerfield is now. Pat Shand had a market garden on the fields straight up from Nelson Street, where Torry Road is now.

Christmas and New Year were very different eighty years ago; there was no holiday for most adults at Christmas, it was just another working day. Christmas trees were practically unknown - I was never at a Christmas party, but the Sunday School might have had a soiree in the Stewarts Hall.

This was a great affair, we got a bag of biscuits as we went in, each bag having precisely the same kind and number of biscuits in it.

There was always a 'German Bun' in that bag; that's what they were called before the 1914-18 War; during the war the name was changed to 'Paris Buns' - I have heard them called 'Bennachies' now for an obvious reason.

The biscuits were washed down with tea from urns - we brought our own cups.Of the entertainment I recall little but we did have a film once, the first that many of us had seen.

New Year's Day was a holiday; just the one day, back to work next day. New Year was THE holiday of the year, when families tried to meet together.

continued on page 29

Alexander Donald, Baker , Duke Street

This a quality family bakery business, founded 130 years ago by the great- grandfather of the present owner, (also Alexander, but known as Sandy like the previous four generations)

The two photographs (page 28) show that amazingly the shop remains unaltered since the building was erected. The top photograph shows the founder of the business flanked by the large staff.

The bakery also had a horse-drawn van which travelled through the town and the country around Huntly. This service has continued down through the ages, ceasing only three years ago in 1993; which is a remarkable indication that people still preferred the personal local service of this particular bakery long after many other rounds had stopped.

Loyal conscientious staff have long been a hallmark of this bakery, amply illustrated by the story of one baker who lived at Rothiemay, cycled in to work every morning for a 4 am start! He would have had to leave his house at some unearthly hour!

Another old photograph held by the family shows on the sign above the door the words "Machine-made", which at the time proved that a local business was prepared to move with the times and invest in equipment to allow expansion. Evidence of the engine house and lineshaft mountings can still be seen in the bakery. Sandy Donald reflects however that the presentday supermarket mentality may finish off local, quality bakers like his.
Let's hope his pessimism is unfounded and that this business will be around for more generations to come.

Sandy Donald (Founder), with his staff outside the shop over 100 years ago.

The Shop front today, unchanged in 130 years.

Boyds Shop pre - 1907 with previous owners.

A typical representative's business card of 1890.

Boyds, Huntly Ltd., 3 The Square

This is a third generation business, each owner known as John Minto Boyd. The business moved to its present location in 1907 from the shop now known as Reid and Gordon. The top photograph (page 29) shows the shop front in the days of the previous owner.

John Boyd, Senior ,set out for Glasgow and Edinburgh to learn his trade in various draperies and outfitting shops, (including "Jenners"!), returning to the family business in 1930.

At one time there were as many as 20 dressmakers in the upstairs rooms awaiting orders from the ladies selecting their materials and patterns in the shop below. Now racks of clothes fill the shop.

The other photograph shows a business card sent by a traveller from the Wholesalers, "Esslemont and McIntosh" to intimate his pending sales visit. No doubt the man arrived by train. Business was certainly more leisurely then.

This very attractive shop with its imposing front, also has an attractive tower at the back, which can be seen from the Bank of Scotland carpark.

The present owner, John Boyd, has expanded the business into carpet fitting and has enlarged the shop out at the back. He is planning to restore the upstair rooms once occupied by the tailors and seamstresses. Boyds have always been prepared to make changes to meet new trading conditions ensuring their success for future generations.

When there was snow about we sledged a lot; the Factory Brae was sometimes crowded with sledges (all home-made) then there might come this dreaded cry "A. B. C. R. L.!" - this was code for " A Bobby Coming, Rin Loons!" - and we all sped away.

The Bobby was sent for now and again to clear us off the Brae - why I know not - there was little traffic to interrupt. I think it was to give them something to do; at that time we had an Inspector, a Sergeant and sometimes six policemen in the town. What they employed themselves at was a mystery, there was less "crime" than there is now, and that is negligible compared with some places.

The Police Station was in Deveron Road; it is still called the Old Police Station.

Come to think of it, it was maybe the abundance of Bobbies that kept the peace - they were always on the beat!

We skated, too, on the Pond in the Plantin, if there was a moon, far into the night. In the evenings when it was too bad to go out it was cards or games - some of us had gramophones.

In place of TV and radio there were Concerts, Whist Drives and Dances (a lot of them). Just before the 1914-18 war a local group produced Gilbert and Sullivan's comic opera. I think people were more sociable then in going out to such entertainments.

The modern way of socialising, going to a pub for a drink and a meal, was totally unknown.

A woman in a pub drinking was a thing unimaginable, and certainly would have been looked upon with a very doubtful eye!

Different days, different ways, I suppose

Another great change today from the days of which I write is the rise in the popularity of Hire-Purchase which was virtually unknown then ; if you wanted something you just saved until you could buy it.
On whether this change is a good thing or not I give no opinion; I merely record the fact.

OCCASIONS

"Feein Market"
One of the highlights of the year was the Feein Market in May, a week before the "Mey Term Day," the 28th. of May.That was the day when farmers and farm servants met to bargain the terms of wages and conditions for the next six months; farm workers were engaged for the half-year.

They were paid no wages until the end of their term; anyone who wanted a "sub" before that was regarded as a "gey thriftless kin o a chiel".

On Feein Market day the Square was crowded with stannies of all kinds; Darts, Roll the Penny, 'Plunky' (home-made toffee), Fruit, Try your Strength (at a penny a time). There was a little mannie with a bowler hat who came every year, carrying his heavy machine up from the station to the Square. "Have a go, Johnnie!" he used to cry. He was reputed to own a street of houses in Aberdeen.

I know for a fact one stall-holder who had a son at University. He ran a "Disc on the Circle" stall at sixpence a try.

Here and there you would see 'Fermers' and 'ferm chiels' locked in commercial combat; when the bargaining was completed the farmer gave his new employee "arles", maybe half-a-crown (twelve and a half new pence!) which sealed the bargain. You got a lot of drink for half-a-crown then, half a dozen bottles of beer, and they generally landed in one of the bars.

This was the first drink that most of these lads had had for six months so it is understandable that some of them were a 'bittie the waar o the weer' towards night.

On their wages they had no choice but be abstemious.

There was an occasional 'fecht' in Sellar's closs but little damage was done; by the time the combatants had got up to fighting pitch in "Klondyke" - the Crown Bar - they could hardly see one another.

I have heard that the Crown Bar got the name of Klondyke because some coins were found when the foundations were being dug in 1898, at the time of the gold rush in Alaska. The 'Gold Rush' started in Alaska when gold was discovered in 1886.

Every farm servant had a bike and Huntly was full of them that day, stacked in every closs and alley.

The Gordon's Band came to the Feein Market recruiting, and many a young chap joined up, inflamed by the skirl of the pipes - and maybe a dram or two - and good Sodgers they made!

I once saw Piper Findlater, VC, of Dargai in the band. In the storming of the Dargai Heights by the Gordons in 1897 he had both legs shattered by bullets. Propped on a stone he kept on playimg until Dargai was taken.

On term day you sometimes saw the carts going through the town carrying all the worldly goods of married men who were flitting to a new job. Single men carried all their possessions in a "timmer" kist. One term day I remember, when it rained the whole day, I saw the carts going down Deveron Street, everything soaked.

Aeroplanes at Huntly

Shortly after the 1914-18 War an aeroplane came to Huntly; from a field on the farm of Thorniebrae it gave short flights, but the charge of fifteen shillings, if I remember aright, was far beyond our reach.

Another came some time later which flew from a field behind the Toll. These early planes were flimsy looking things. This one was a biplane, wings and body made of canvas over a frame and seemingly held together by wires. I was up in that one, ten bob it cost me (fifty pence!); a fortune!

To get in you went up little portable steps and threw a leg over the edge and sat - crouched rather - behind the pilot. Another passenger sat behind you in the same way; it was quite open, you just rested your arm on the edge and looked over and down at the country below.

What struck one about these early planes, apart from the novelty of looking down at the country below, was the noise and the wind; if you stuck your head out from behind the shelter of the pilot (who had on a leather coat and helmet plus goggles) your breath was taken away. It may not have looked it from the ground but actually we were going faster than an express train.

You don't get that exhilarating experience on a plane now - though you still get cramped up!

Circuses

Great was the excitment and anticipation when the gaudy bills went up in the shop windows, on the telephone poles, everywhere, announcing that a circus was coming to town.

Pinder, Pinder-Ord, Lord John Sanger, these were the names we were familiar with; 'Lord' John wasn't in the Peerage, he just gave himself that fore-name.

Inside the big top the performance was much the same as now; horses, elephants, the big cats, gymnasts and so on.

The big difference between the circus then and now was the transport; the wagons were hauled by teams of tough little horses and you had to get up early in the morning if you wanted to see them coming onto their stance on the Muir. They travelled through the night if the performance was next day.

The Circuses were proud of their horses. After their job was done they were stabled in a long tent where the public could go in and see them and a fine sight it was.

There were piebalds, chestnuts, bays munching away at their hay, all in beautiful condition, with glossy skins you could shave at.

Some of the circuses had a procession through the town before the performance, ladies in their spangles on horseback, elephants, clowns stiltmen.

George Stephen, the chemist, (Stewart now) was standing outside his door watching the procession going past; a stiltman called out, "How are you Mr Stephen? Long time since I've seen you!"

The people wondered how he knew Mr Stephen so well; he didn't - he just read his name on the sign above the door!

In the days of which I write Huntly had a Town Council with Provost and Baillies, and I wish we had one again; local affairs are better dealt with locally. We are too far from Government now and the ordinary citizen feels a sense of impotence; his complaints are too often addressed apparently to a stone wall.

Elections for the Town Council were usually pretty keen affairs, the aspirants being all local, of course, and well known to everybody. After the Council was elected there was the ceremony of the "Kirkin o the Council" when the Council marched in a body, in frock coats and lum hats, to the Kirk, presumably to ask a blessing on their work in the ensuing term of office! The last meeting of the Council before the next election was known the "Greetin Meetin" for obvious reasons - some Councillors might not be re-elected!

There used to be a curious custom on Polling night; a flaming barrel was rolled round the streets by the loons, that is until the bobbies caught up with them.

What the origin of this custom was I do not know; I'm tempted to think that it goes back to tribal times when perhaps the departed Chief was cremated before the election of his successor! This may sound bizarre, but many of these old customs have very deep roots.

Housewife's Choice

Some folk yearn for 'the Good Old Days'; let us describe one of them.

Let us suppose a young Housewife to be wafted back in time to the period of which I have written.

It's winter and Monday morning.

She gets up early, very early because it's washing day!)There is an unwritten law that washing has to be done on Monday; why I don't know)

The house is cold, really cold; (no central heating then, remember!). First thing our Heroine lights a candle, left handy near the bed, and gropes her way to the kitchen. There she lights the gas, if she has it; if not a paraffin lamp.

Next thing is to get the fire going; she probably has a range, a great black coal eater which has a fire box and an oven, and a flat top which kept things hottish once they are cooked.

The fire-bar has to be rattled to get the ashes into the ash-pan below, then the stones picked out from the fire box - the quantity depending on your coalman - then the half-burned bits of coal, which are laid aside.

Now comes the laying of the fire; screwed up newspapers are put in first, then dry sticks, then the half-burnt bits, then small bits of coal. You light the paper from below and hope for the best.

The range has a boiler at the back which heats water, given time!

There is a 'hob', a round hole with a lid on, on the flat top of the range above the fire box on which the kettle, pan or whatever is placed, with the lid off, of course. All the cooking is done on this one hob; there are bars in front of the fire box, covered by a swinging door to keep in the heat, - that's where the toasting is done.

It helps if everyone likes the same kind of meal; they usually have to!

Breakfast over, the man of the house off to work and the bairns to school, now comes the washing.

The wash-house is outside, generally a lean-to or a sheddie at the back of the house to hold the boiler and the sinks. The boiler is a big affair with a fire underneath and a lum sticking through the roof.

A provident housewife will lay the fire the night before to save time in the morning.

Often as not the boiler has to filled by carrying water from the house. Emptying is a laborious business by means of a 'dipper', a small pan.

A successful washing day has to be dry, of course, but much depends on the wind; if it's in the wrong airt the lum won't draw, the fire won't burn and the water won't heat.

On such a day menfolk will know to keep well out of sight and sound!

We will suppose though, that everything has gone well; things are washed and rinsed in the sink and ready to hang out on the line. Very pleasant and satisfying it is to see a line of washing flapping away in the sun and a fine drying wind, but the battle is not yet won.

Anxious eyes scan the Heavens for any sign of rain; at the first drop a rush is made with the big clothes basket to get things down before the good work of the sun and wind is undone.

The shower past, everything has to be hung out again; this may happen more than once and sorely tests the temperament of the hanger-out!

In anticipation of such calamities the prudent housewife makes a pact with a neighbour; in an emergency, maybe having to fly down to the shop for 'something ti the tea', and the rain coming on whilst she is away, the neighbour will rush to the rescue. We have known a gap left permanently in a fence for that purpose!

We'll suppose the day has been a success and the harvest is safely gathered in, the washing dry and in the basket ready for the iron.

It can be understood that Monday is not a day for callers, not until the things are dry and in; that is when the neighbours, also flushed with success, will gather for a triumphal cup!

Ironing is done in the evening after tea-time is over, and it is a more leisurely business, the anxieties of the day a memory. Ironing is not without a spice of danger; the box iron is hollow with a sliding lid at the back into which a 'heater' is dropped.

The heater is a lump of iron which is heated in the fire; it has a hole in the wide end into which the poker is inserted (after it has been located!) and is liable to fall off prematurely while being lifted out

I entitled this piece "Housewife's Choice" but I don't suppose many housewives today would choose to give up their present conveniences and go back to the twenties!

But every advantage has a disadvantage, and it may be that the gain in ease in performing household tasks is counterbalanced by a loss in job satisfaction, a precious thing, not always to be attained by pressing a switch.

A lady once told me of the therapeutic virtues of the washing tub. These were not her words exactly; what she said was, "There's naethin like up ti the oxters in het soapy watter an layin intil a fool sark ti get redd o yir ill-naiter!"

I know from my own experience that the emptying from the tumble-drier of creased, half-warm stuff does not give the same satisfaction as the filling the clothes basket from a flapping line of snowy, wind-won whites.

I have enlarged on an aulden day washing as illustrative of the great change in domestic affairs since the coming of electricity.

I will end with the words of Sir Roger de Coverly, on an occasion requiring diplomacy, "There is much to be said on both sides!"

Epilogue

If I were asked what is the greatest visual change I see in Huntly now from the town of three-quarters of a century ago, I would say the extent of new building, and the huge increase of traffic on the streets.

To the South beyond the Muir and the Hospital there were just green fields; to the West of King Street the only building in sight on the Torry was Pat Shand's sheddie, from which he dispensed tatties and cabbages from his Market Garden on what is now Torry Road.

There were no houses south of Bleachfield Street, and the Green Road was just that, a country roadie meandering through the old bleach fields, down to Brander's Mill.

The railway lines are still there, but the trains, once the only means of transport over long distances are few and far between, ousted by the bus, but mainly by the car.

The motor car, like fire, is a good servant but a bad master; essential now for many purposes, its steadily increasing numbers have made for a reduction in the quality of life in every City and Town; remembering the quiet streets and roads of my youth, I am quite sure of that.

There have been many changes in the town since the twenties - some for the better, some not - but in one thing I find no change; the Fowk! They are still the same friendly, helpful people they have always been, and if I may venture to prophesy, always will be!

Introduction to the Appendices

APPENDIX 1

The column on the left is a list of Traders in the 1920s with their addresses.
The column on the right is the present Occupier of these premises.

APPENDIX 2

For this Appendix I had a walk round the town.
In the column on the left are the present occupiers of the premises.
In the column on the right are the occupiers in the Twenties.

The Appendices complement one another. These tables are constructed from memory so perhaps any errors or omissions will be excused

Appendix 1

Businesses in Huntly

75 Years Ago		Now
Bakers		
A. Donald	Duke Street	*No change*
J. Ewen	Deveron Street	Work Wear
J. Gordon	Gordon Street	Smith, Baker
A. Grant	Deveron Street	*Empty (late Deans)*
J. Kennedy	Bogie Street	House No 17
C. Murdoch	Gordon Street	R.G Mitchell, Gen. Merchant
D. Niven	Gordon Street	D. Wright, Saddler
J. Stephen	Bogie Street	House No 37
Banks		
Commercial	Gordon Street	Stewart, Chemist
North of Scotland	Gordon Street	Council
North of Scotland	The Square	The Clydesdale
The Royal	Duke Street	C.A.,(*to be a teashop*)
Booksellers		
Harry McConnachie	The Square	Menzies
A. McKenzie	Duke Street	Huntly Launderette
George McLennan	Duke Street	W. Bruce, Newsagent
Builders		
A. Drummond	East Park Street	*not trading*
R. J. Logie	Church Street	*not trading*
F. MacIntosh	Gordon Street	*not trading*
P. R. Mitchell	East Park Street	*not trading*
Simpson & Lipp	Upperkirkgate	*not trading*

	75 Years Ago	Now

Butchers

Name	Street	Now
C. Anderson	Gordon Street	Ex-Servicemen's Club
Barron & Duffton	Deveron Street	House No 28
Gordon Rhind	Gordon Street	Rural Support Service
John Rhind	4 Bogie Street	Huntly Saw Services
James Scott	Duke Street	Watt &Jordan Optician

Chemists

Name	Street	Now
Adam Gilchrist	Duke Street	Bagrie, Electrician
John Raffan	Duke Street	Baird, Chemist
Charles Rule	Duke Street	Empty (*last occupant Reid Flory, Chemist)*
George Stephen	Gordon Street	Stewart, Chemist

China Shop

Name	Street	Now
Mrs McKenzie	Bogie Street	Forbes Raeburn

Chip Shops

Name	Street	Now
Innes	Bogie Street	Demolished
Lundie	Deveron Street	Demolished(*now street parking)*

Confectioners

Name	Street	Now
Sievewright	Deveron Street	Empty(*last occupant Featch, DIY)*
"Birdie" Martin	Nelson Street	E. Mearns, Electrician
Annie Mutch	Castle Street	Smith, Baker
Miss Annie Smith	Castle Street	Public Toilets
Aurileo Amadei ("Riley") (First icecream shop)	Gordon Street	Rizza's, Icecream and Confections

Cycle Agents

Name	Street	Now
McCabe	Bogie Street	Anderson, Grocer
Fitzpatrick	Duke Street	Red Cross
Dick Mitchell	Deveron Street	J. Scarborough
Morrison	Gordon Street	*(Part of Cockburn' s shoe shop)*
Bob Whyte	Duke Street	'Your Choice', Gift Shop

	75 Years Ago	Now
Dairies		
The Buttercup	Gordon Street	Webster, Photographer
Peter Reid	Meadow Street	House No 53
John Wilson	The Square	The Royal Bank
Dentists		
Greig Hughes	Bogie Street	Flat, *(above Huntly Pet Shop)*
J. McKay	Duke Street	Stewart & McCulloch Dentists
Drapers		
J.M.Boyd	The Square	*No change*
Dawson	Duke Street	Food Store (Co-op)
Fordyce	Duke Street	'Dress Sense'
A. Fraser	Duke Street	Huntly Golf Shop
William Gray	Gordon Street	Stewarts Hall, (North Wing)
W. Ingram	Bogie Street	Huntly Pet Shop
Reid & Gordon	Gordon Street	*No change*
Fancy Goods		
Miss Jessie Stewart	The Square	'Square Deal'
Fish Shops		
J. Gardiner	The Square	The Royal Bank
John Paterson	Duke Street	'Nero's', Hairdresser
Mrs Watt	Gordon Street	'Dragon Garden', Chip-shop
Garages		
Archibald	Nelson Street	Late Archie McRailt
Fitzpatrick	Gordon Street	Behind Tele-radio
Green-grocers		
D. H. Niven	Bogie Street	House No 61
Belle Turner	Gordon Street	'Just Hair'
Grocers		
J. Anderson	Gordon Street	Burnett T.V.
Mrs Bain	Deveron Street	House No 4
W. McKenzie	Bogie Street	Forbes Raeburn
J. R. Donald	Gordon Street	Huntly Gallery

43

Grocers(continued)

Howieson	Old Road	'Moneywise'
Goerge Robertson	Gordon Street	Cockburn, Shoes
McConnachie	Bogie Street	*Empty*
D. McKenzie	Deveron Street	R.A. Munro, Architect
Seivewright	Deveron Street	*Empty (Late Featch, DIY)*
Watt Bros.	The Square	'Alldays'
John Wilson	The Square	T.S.B.
Mrs Young	Church Street	House
A. B. Yule	Bogie Street	'Jackies', Hairdresser

Hairdressers

James Donnelly	Duke Street	Baird, Chemist
Bill Rice	The Square	The Royal Bank
Miss Turner	Gordon Street	'Just Hair'

Ironmongers

Cruickshank	The Square	*No change*
A & F Stephen	Duke Street	*No change*

Icecream Shop
(*first icecream shop*)

"Riley"	Gordon Street	Rizza's
(Aurileo Amadei)		

Jam Factory

A. Dufton	Bogie Street	Chip Shop

Joiners

Duncan Davidson	Deveron Street	House (No. 29)
J. McKay	King Street	Robson, Joiner & Undertaker
A. Shewan	Queen Street	House

Leather Merchant

J. & G. Arnott	The Square	TV Services & Sheltered Housing

75 Years Ago		Now
Library	The Square	*No change*
Market Gardeners		
A. Johnston	Gordon Street	Pine Antiques
D. H. Niven	Bogie Street	House (No. 61)
Pat Shand	The Torry	Houses (Scott Drive Area)
Milliners		
Miss Burns	Duke Street	'Oscars', Pet Shop
Diack	Gordon Street	Strathbogie Tele-Radio
Miss Duncan	The Square	Scottish Building Society
Mill Wrights		
A. Dey	Church Street	Council Housing
Needlework		
Miss Morgan	Duke Street	Huntly Antiques
Painters		
E. Ewan	Nelson Street	House
G. Lobban	Castle Street	Robertson, Decorators
George Mitchell	Queen Street	New Bungalows
Hector Mitchell	Gordon Street	Ex-Servicemens' Club
Mitchell	Bogie Street	Sim's, Shoemaker
Pawn Shop		
Calder	Gordon Street	Forbes Sports Shop
Photographers		
W. Clark	Duke Street	Demolished (*carpark for the Rose and Thistle*)
J. Kilgour	Granary Street	G Cruickshanks & Son Sculptors
Plumbers		
R. Douglas	Castle Street	House No 24
John Wilson	Granary Street	Huntly Cycle Centre

75 Years Ago		Now
"Plunkey" Maker		
Mrs Stuart	Duke Street	'The Lunch Box'
(Homemade Toffee)		
Post Office	The Square	*No change (enlarged 1934)*
Printers		
The Huntly Express	Duke Street	The Card Shop
J. Munro	Bogie Street	Grant, Printer
Saddlers		
Gray-Shewan	Duke Street	Linden Sports
Sculptor		
Boddie- Gordon	Bogie Street	Late Duffus
Shoemakers		
A. Alexander	Duke Street	New Teashop
J. Cattenach	Castle Street	Castle Cafe
Joe Dawson	Deveron Street	L.L.Ingram (Stewart)
G. Duncan	Gordon Street	Economic Stores
Dunns	Duke Street	Huntly Carpets
Mutch Bros.	Duke Street	Auto Spares
W. Petrie	Bogie Street	*Empty (late Gauld's)*
J. Wright	Gordon Street	Alliance & Leicester, Building Society
Slaters		
Cowans	Bogie Street	*demolished*
Tailors		
W. Charles	Deveron Street	'Work Wear'
Adam Chree	Bogie Street	Penny Royal
George Clark	The Square	Tourist Information
Sam Copland	Bogie Street	House
J. Murray	Bogie Street	Clark, Hardy & Co., CA
Stuart	Gordon Street	Manus Ward, Jeweller

	75 Years Ago	Now
Tinsmiths		
Bowman-Thain	The Square	*(lane between 'Square Deal' and Cullen Court)*
Tobacconists		
Mrs Fitzpatrick	Duke Street	Red Cross
Watchmakers		
A. Anton	Duke Street	Fred Watt, (Webster)
Peter Shand	Golden Square	House
A. Simpson	Duke Street	New Teashop
J. Watt	Duke Street	Watt & Milligan, Optician
Wholesale Merchants		
Mellis	Gordon Street	Gordon & Innes
Wool Shops		
Brander's,	Bogie Street	House (No. 39)
Ingram	Nelson Street	Houses No.s 5 - 7
Stephen's Wool Mill	Station Road	*Empty (houses being built)*

Appendix 2

"A Walk around the Town"

The Square (clockwise)

Now	Then
Gordon Arms	*No change*
Car parking space	Gordon's Temperance Hotel
Cruickshanks	*No change*
Denim Plus	Part of Cruickshanks
TV Services	Arnott,s Shoe Factory
Square Deal	Miss Stewart, Fancy Goods
Huntly Hotel	*No change*
Library	*No change*
Post Office	*No change (enlarged 1934)*
Royal Bank	Commercial Bank
	W. Rice, Barber
Tourist Information	George Clark, Tailor
Scottish Building Society	Miss Duncan, Milliner
TSB	John Wilson, Grocer
Cockburn's Coffee Shop	Wilson's store
Menzies	Harry McConnachie, Newsagent
J. M. Boyd	*No change*
Clydesdale Bank	North of Scotland Bank

Duke Street (North side from the Square)

Now	Then
Red Cross	Mrs Fitzpatrick, Tobacconist
	J. Fitzpatrick, Cycles
Watt, Ironmonger	Stephen, Ironmonger
Linden Sports	Shewan, Saddler
Card Shop	Huntly Express
Baird, Chemist	Raffan, Chemist
	J. Cowie, Confectioner
	J. Donelly, Barber
Nero's, Hairdresser	John Paterson, Fish Shop

Now	Then
R. W. Bagrie, Electrician	Adam Gilchrist, Chemist
Bruce, Newsagent	McLennan, Newsagent
Roy Brodie, Bookmaker	*Part of the Royal Oak*
Royal Oak	*No change*
Moneywise	W. Howieson, Grocer
Your Choice	Bob Whyte
Rose & Thistle carpark	Clark, Photographer
Rose & Thistle	*No change*

Bogie Street,(North Side from the Square)

Now	Then
Marshall's Garage	Wordie's Yard
MacDonald, Plumber	Wordie's Office
Duffus Monumental Mason	Peter Gordon, Monumental Mason
Chip Shop	A. Dufton, Grocer and Jam Factory
Anderson, Grocer	McCabe, Cycles
Empty shop(late Gauld)	Petrie, Shoemaker
Empty shop No 23	McConnachie, Confectioner
Cruickshank & Son, Sculptor	Kilgour, Photographer
Building Alteration	John Rhind's slaughter house

Duke Street, (South Side from the Square)

Now	Then
Strathbogie Bakery	John Wilson's Dairy
The Lunch Box	Mrs Stuart, 'Plunky' (home-made toffee)
Milligan, Optician	John Watt, Watchmaker
Dress Sense	Fordyce, Draper
Huntly Golf Shop	A. Frase, Draper
Scott, Butcher	McCabe, Cycles
Teashop (late C.A.)	The Royal Bank
	Simpson, Watchmaker
Murdoch, McMath & Mitchell Solicitors	*No change*
Donald, Baker	*No change*
Fred Watt (Webster), Jeweller	A. Anton, Watchmaker
Empty shop (late Reid Flory)	R. Dufton, Chemist (R. Dufton opened a Toffee Factory in McDonald Street where Huntly Motor Cycles now is)

Duke Street (South side from the Square) (*continued*)

Now	Then
Huntly Carpet Centre	Dunn, Shoemaker
Huntly Launderette	A. MacKenzie, Bookseller
Huntly Antiques	Miss Morgan, Needlework
Oscar, Pet Shop	Miss Burns, Milliner
Autospares	Mutch Bros., Shoemakers
Watt & Jordan, Opticians	Jas. Scott, Butcher
Foodstore (Co-op)	Dawson, Draper

Bogie Street (South side from the Square)

Now	Then
Huntly Pet Shop	W. McKenzie, Grocer
Hydro Board Shop	W. Ingram, Draper
Forbes Raeburn, Butcher	Miss McKenzie, Grocer
Huntly Music	Miss McKenzie, China
Penny Royal	Adam Chree, Tailor
Hair & Beauty	House
House (No 17)	Kennedy, Baker
Huntly Saw Services	John Rhind, Butcher
J. Sim, Boots & Shoes	Mitchell, Painter
J. Grant, Printer	Munro, Printer
Clark, Hardy & Co., C.A.s	Murray, Tailor
House (No 37)	J. Stephen, Baker
House (No 39)	Brander's Wool Shop
Strathbogie Hotel	*No change*
Jackie, Hairdresser	A. B. Yule, Merchant & Seedsman

Gordon Street (East side from the Square)

Now	Then
Bank of Scotland	Union Bank
The Crown Bar	*No change*
Alliance & Liecester	Wight, Shoe repairer
Stewart, Chemist	Commercial Bank
Stewart Chemist	George Stephen, Chemist
Cost Cutter (Esson)	The Cinema (Palais de Luxe)
Rizza's	Aurileo Amadei (Riley), Icecream
Barnett TV	J. Anderson, Grocer
Workshop (Pictures)	Gordon, Travel Agent

Gordon Street (East side from the Square)

Now	Then
Chaps Barber	Rod Rice, Barber
J. Rhind (Raeburn)	House
Flair (Rosier)	Frank MacIntosh, Builder
Huntly Gallery	J. R. Donald, Grocer
Job Centre	Gordon Rhind, Butcher
Just Hair	Belle Turner, Greengrocer
	Miss Turner, Hairdresser
Gordon & Innes	Mellis, Wholesalers
Cockburn, Shoemaker	Robertson, Grocer
(part of above premises)	Morrison's cycles
R. G. Mitchell, Gen. Merchant	Charlie Murdoch, Baker
Pine Antiques	Johnstone, Market Gardener

Gordon Street, (West side from the Square)

Now	Then
Alldays	J. & J. Watt, Grocers
Strathbogie Tele-Radio	Diack, Draper
G. Webster, Photographer	Buttercup Dairy
Huntly Express Office	F. A. B. Mitchell, Solicitor
	(later Mitchell & Middleton)
Manus Ward, Jeweller	Stuart, Tailor
North wing of Stewart's Hall	W. Gray, Draper
(eyelets for blinds still visible above the windows!)	
Economic Stores	Duncan, Shoemaker
Reid & Gordon, Drapers	*No change*
Aberdeenshire Council	North of Scotland Bank
Dragon Garden Chip Shop	Mrs Watt, Fishmonger
Picture House (*empty*)	House
Donald Wright, Saddler	Niven, Baker
Vet's Surgery	Tenement
Forbes's Sports Shop	Calder's Pawn Shop
Smith, Baker	James Gordon, Grocer & Baker
G.R.A.I.N.	James Gordon, Grocer & Baker
Ex-Servicemen's Club	Charlie Anderson, Butcher
	Mrs. M. A. Reid, Confectioner
Watt's Garage	House
Spences Knitwear Factory*(closed)*	*No change*
Tony's Restaurant *(closed)*	The Lemon Tree Inn

Deveron Street (South side from Square)

Now	Then
Car Parking Space	Gordon's Temperance Hotel
Workwear	J. Ewen, Baker
	Charles, Tailor
Scarborough, Electrician	Dick Mitchell, Cycles, Handyman
House	Barron & Dufton, Butchers
House (No 4)	Mrs Bain (*later Smith*) Grocer
Empty Shop	Grant, Baker

Deveron Street, (North side from the Square)

Now	Then
L. L. Ingram (Stewart)	Joe Dawson, Shoe Repairer
Strath Deveron Hotel	*No change*
Pet Shop (*closed*)	Mrs Scott, Cold Meat, etc.
R. A. Munro, Architect	Danny McKenzie, Grocer
Handyman Supplies (*empty*)	Sievewright, Confectioner
Smiddy (*closed*)	Wilson, Blacksmith

Castle Street, (West side from the Square)

Now	Then
Public Toilets	Miss Annie Smith, Confectioner
Robertson, Decorator	Lobban, Painter
Smith, Baker	Annie Mutch, Confectioner
Hair (Elizabeth Jane)Fashions	House

Castle Street, (West side from the Square)

Now	Then
Castle Cafe	Cattenach, Shoe Repairer
Police Station	Tenements ("Fairyland")
Council Flats	Chip Shop